THE OFFICIAL
TOTTENH...
HOTSPUR™
ANNUAL 2008

Written by David Clayton
Designed by Simon Thorley

g

A Grange Publication

ISBN 978-1-905426-94-2

£6.99

CONTENTS

PREMIERSHIP REVIEW 2006/2007

Much was expected of Spurs for the 2006/2007 Premiership season and hopes were high, so a good, solid start would be crucial...

AUGUST

Pld: 3 W: 1 D: 0 L: 2 F: 2 A: 4

Bolton (a)
Sheff Utd (h)
Everton (h)

The arrival of Bulgarian Dimitar Berbatov for £10.9m was undoubtedly the signing that most excited the Spurs fans. Didier Zokora and Pascal Chimbonda also moved to White Hart Lane in high profile deals, with Michael Carrick moving to Manchester United for a fee in excess of £18m. With many of the squad returning from international duty just days before the start of the new campaign, it was perhaps no surprise that Bolton took full advantage of a disjointed Spurs and register a 2-0 win. Berbatov took just seven minutes of his home debut to open his account in the next match against Sheffield United and Jermaine Jenas added a second to seal a 2-0 victory. With another home game against Everton just a few days later, it was vital to make it back-to-back home wins but it proved to be a frustrating afternoon at the Lane as the visitors, reduced to 10 men, recorded a surprise 2-0 win.

SEPTEMBER

Pld: 3 W: 0 D: 1 L: 2 F: 0 A: 4

Man Utd (a)
Fulham (h)
Liverpool (a)

A goal from Ryan Giggs was enough to give Manchester United a 1-0 win at Old Trafford. Three points from nine meant Fulham at home was a must-win match for Martin Jol's side, but the Cottagers left with a 0-0 draw. Worse was to follow with a comprehensive 3-0 defeat at Liverpool leaving Spurs fourth bottom with just four points from a possible 18 – at least six points less than many would have expected from the opening fixtures.

OCTOBER

Pld: 4 W: 2 D: 2 L: 0 F: 4 A: 2

Portsmouth (h)
Aston Villa (a)
West Ham (h)
Watford (a)

Spurs took just 39 seconds to breach Portsmouth's defence with an intelligent back-heel from Danny Murphy. A second from Defoe was just enough to relieve the pressure on the manager and team and despite Kanu's header reducing the lead, Spurs won 2-1. A point at Martin O'Neill's Aston Villa continued the improvement in form with Villa striker Juan Pablo Angel missing a penalty for the hosts then scoring an own goal minutes later! Gareth Barry earned the Midlands outfit a draw with a terrific strike but a first point on the road was still welcomed. A fine individual goal from Mido saw off West Ham at White Hart Lane though the 0-0 draw at Watford was seen as two points lost rather than one gained. At least it maintained an upturn in form away from the Lane.

NOVEMBER

Pld: 4 W: 2 D: 1 L: 1 F: 7 A: 6

Chelsea (h)
Reading (a)
Blackburn (a)
Wigan (h)

November couldn't have begun any better with a win – at last – over reigning champions Chelsea. Makelele gave the visitors the lead but Michael Dawson scored a cracking header to level matters. The winner came from Aaron Lennon after good work by Keane to end a 16-year wait to beat our London rivals. There was yet more disappointment away from the Lane with a 3-1 defeat at Reading and a 1-1 draw at Blackburn meaning that for all the good work being done at home, the failure to win away was pegging the team back. It was a relief to see off Wigan 3-1 on home soil to end the month on a high, thanks to goals from Defoe, Berbatov and Lennon.

DECEMBER

Pld: 7 W: 4 D: 0 L: 3 F:12 A: 11

Arsenal (a)
Middlesbrough (h)
Charlton (h)
Manchester City (a)
Newcastle (a)
Aston Villa (h)
Liverpool (h)

The North London derby ended in misery as Arsenal recorded a 3-0 win in the first clash between the sides at the Emirates Stadium, but a 2-1 home win over Middlesbrough put the smile back on the Spurs fans' faces with Berbatov scoring a blistering volley and Keane grabbing a later winner. A 5-1 win over struggling Charlton pushed the Lilywhites further up the Premiership table with goals from Berbatov (2), Tainio, Steed Malbranque and Defoe – it was the perfect morale-booster with the busy Christmas period looming. Spurs celebrated Martin Jol's one hundredth game in charge by ending their away jinx at a ground where the pickings have been rich in recent years – the City of Manchester Stadium where goals from Calum Davenport and a howitzer from Tom Huddlestone secured a 2-1 win over Manchester City. It was a case of normal service resumed in the next Premiership game with a 3-1 loss at Newcastle undoing the good work done in Manchester. A 2-1 Boxing Day win over Aston Villa, thanks to two goals from Defoe, made it seven home wins in a row, but four days later Liverpool left the Lane with all three points thanks to Xabi Alonso's solitary strike. Going into the New Year, Spurs were eighth in the table, leaving Jol's men nicely placed for a European push.

JANUARY

Pld: 3 W: 0 D: 2 L: 1 F: 4 A: 5

Portsmouth (a)
Newcastle (h)
Fulham (a)

A point away to Portsmouth was a decent way to start 2007 with Malbranque's header earning a deserved draw at Fratton Park, but a second successive home defeat - despite twice being ahead against Newcastle - deflated the feel-good factor at White Hart Lane. Many more home losses and European qualification would become all-but impossible. Fulham again proved a tough nut to crack and it took Pascal Chimbonda's first goal for the club to earn a 1-1 draw at Craven Cottage.

FEBRUARY

Pld: 4 W: 2 D: 0 L: 2 F: 7 A: 8

Manchester Utd (h)
Sheffield United (a)
Everton (a)
Bolton (h)

A 4-0 home defeat to a rampant Manchester United severely dented Spurs' UEFA Cup hopes and a 2-1 loss away to Sheffield United suggested a return to the Lilywhites' bad old ways on the road. It also meant no Premiership wins in six. A win at Everton, also chasing European qualification became crucial to how the season would pan out and goals from Berbatov and Jermaine Jenas gave Spurs arguably their most impressive victory away from home so far and it was followed up by another terrific win over UEFA Cup rivals Bolton, who were sent back to the north-west with a 4-1 thrashing against their name.

MARCH

Pld: 2 W: 2 D: 0 L: 0 F: 7 A: 4

West Ham (a)
Watford (h)

A thrilling London derby at West Ham saw Spurs fight back from 2-0 down to win a cracking game 4-3. Jermain Defoe pulled a goal back from the spot and Tainio smashed home a shot from the edge of the box to make it 2-2. The Hammers went ahead again but further strikes from Berbatov and Paul Stalteri – the latter in injury time – completed a breathless encounter. The next Premiership match – at home to Watford – saw Jenas put Spurs 1-0 up with a header but the goal of the game came when Paul Robinson's 80-yard free kick found its way into the Hornets' net for an unforgettable goal for the England keeper. Hossam Ghaly completed the scoring in a 3-1 win.

APRIL

Pld: 5 W: 2 D: 2 L: 1 F: 9 A: 8

Reading (h)
Chelsea (a)
Wigan (a)
Arsenal (h)
Middlesbrough (a)

A 1-0 win over Reading pushed Spurs up to seventh in the table. It seemed that Jol's men were timing their push for a UEFA Cup spot to perfection. A 1-0 defeat at Chelsea was followed by an exciting 3-3 draw away to Wigan, with an equaliser from Jermaine Jenas earning a vital point and there was another thrilling draw in the return derby with Arsenal. Keane put Spurs ahead but the Gunners fought back to lead 2-1 – it took a 94th minute equaliser to make it 2-2. A 3-2 win at Middlesbrough confirmed the Keane/Berbatov partnership as one of the best in the Premiership with both men scoring the goals and the pair would later be voted the Premiership players of the month.

MAY

Pld: 3 W: 2 D: 1 L: 0 F: 5 A: 2

Charlton (a)
Blackburn (h)
Man City (h)

There was still ground to be made on teams above Spurs in the table if a top six finish was to be achieved and a stunning goal from – who else? – Dimitar Berbatov paved the way for a 2-0 win at the Valley and Defoe sealed the points while relegating Charlton at the same time. Spurs then ended Blackburn's UEFA Cup dreams with a 1-1 draw at the Lane, courtesy of Defoe's 18th goal of the campaign, and a hard-fought 2-1 win over Manchester City confirmed European football for a second successive season. Keane and Berbatov – fittingly – scored the goals to complete a very satisfying season with much more to come in 2007/2008.

SPURS IN EUROPE 2006/2007

A bit more luck and the Lilywhites might have gone all the way to the UEFA Cup final last season, but reaching the last eight was no mean feat...

Away Venue: Stadion Evzena Rosickeho, Prague

UEFA Cup 1, Leg 1:
Slavia Prague 0 Spurs 1
UEFA Cup 1, Leg 2:
Spurs 1, Slavia Prague 0
(Spurs win 2-0 on aggregate)

There's nothing quite like an away match in Europe and the Spurs fans who followed the team to Prague to take on Slavia enjoyed the journey from start to finish. With Martin Jol's side having a very cosmopolitan look about them, they were tipped in some quarters as one of the tournament's dark horses and when Jermaine Jenas scored a vital away goal on 37 minutes, the adventure had really begun. Slavia applied pressure after the break but the balance had tipped firmly in the visitors' favour and Spurs returned to North London with 1-0 lead.

The second leg was perhaps more tense than it should have been and it took a Robbie Keane goal on 80 minutes – his first of the season – to settle the capacity White Hart Lane crowd.

Venue: Inonu Stadium, Besiktas

UEFA Cup, Group B:
Besiktas 0 Spurs 2

A potentially tricky start to the group stages of the UEFA Cup was negotiated smoothly by a Spurs side who couldn't buy a win away from home in the Premiership, yet were anything but a pushover on their European travels. Besiktas, managed by former Fulham boss Jean Tigana, had never beaten an English side in European competition and when Hossam Ghaly scored his first goal for Spurs on 31 minutes, the Turkish fans knew they were going to have to wait even longer for their jinx to end. Exactly 31 minutes later Dimitar Berbatov collected a ball from Keane, lost his marker before rounding the keeper and making it 2-0. Game, set and match!

Venue:
White Hart Lane

UEFA Cup, Group B:
Spurs 3, Club Brugge 1

It was Belgian opposition for Spurs in the next Group B clash and the visitors quickly registered their intent by going close after just two minutes. Whereas that attack resulted in a great save by Paul Robinson, the England keeper could do nothing about Salou Ibrahim's fierce drive on 13 minutes that put Brugge 1-0 up. The hosts quickly levelled matters when a move involving Pascal Chimbonda and Jermaine Jenas presented a chance to Berbatov who hammered home the equlaiser. The second goal didn't come until the 62nd minute, but when it did, it was well worth the wait with Berbatov setting Keane free and the Irish international finishing clinically with a crisp shot. Berbatov sealed the victory on 72 minutes with a smart header from Ghaly's cross and leaving Spurs looking good to progress into the knock-out rounds with maximum points from their opening two group games.

Venue:
Bay Arena, Leverkusen

UEFA Cup, Group B:
Bayer Leverkusen 0 Spurs 1

Spurs made it three away wins on the trot in Europe despite not having won any of their seven Premiership away games up to that point. Leverkusen have a reputation as one of European football's most consistent performers in recent times but in truth, Jol's men should have won by two or three goals on the night. With Berbatov returning to the club he'd left just months earlier, it was perhaps predictable that the Bulgarian would return to haunt his former employers and on 34 minutes, he did exactly that, finishing from close range after Aaron Lennon had been denied. Spurs were rampant after the break and ultimately the German side were fortunate to escape with just a single goal defeat.

Venue:
White Hart Lane

UEFA Cup, Group B:
Spurs 3, Dinamo Bucharest 1

Another entertaining evening at the Lane as Spurs dismantled a useful Bucharest side with a minimum of fuss. It was that man Berbatov again who opened the scoring on 15 minutes with a stunning shot into the top right corner of the visitors' net. An impressive individual goal by Jermain Defoe made it 2-0 on 38 minutes and the same player scored four minutes after the break to seal the victory. Mendy pulled one back in injury time but with a one hundred per cent record in the group stage, Spurs marched into the knock-out rounds in a confident manner.

UEFA Cup, Round of 16,
Leg 1: SC Braga 2 Spurs 3
UEFA Cup, Round of 16,
Leg 2: Spurs 3 SC Braga 2
(Spurs win 6-4 on aggregate)

A pulsating first leg in Portugal was eventually settled by a late Spurs winner - after we had thown away a 2-0 lead. With the first half failing to ignite, it was skipper Keane who opened the scoring on 57 minutes with a delightful dipping volley and Steed Malbranque made it 2-0 14 minutes later. Braga finally awoke and forced a penalty three minutes later, but despite Robinson saving the spot-kick, Jorge scored from the rebound. Ze Carlos made it 2-2 on 81 minutes and from looking a certain away win, Spurs now had to ensure they didn't leave with a defeat, but Keane's last gasp strike made it 3-2 to restore the visitor's advantage.

The second leg was another five goal thriller with Braga levelleing aggregate scores on 25 minutes through Luis Filipe, but Berbatov scored his sixth European goal just three minutes later to make it 1-1. The same player made it 2-1 with an incredible volley on 41 minutes but the plucky Portuguese refused to lie down and made it 2-2 through Andrade just before the hour mark was reached. Berbatov was the goal provider, however, for Malbranque on 75 minutes to complete the scoring and send Spurs into the quarter-finals.

Away Venue: Ramon Sanchez-Pizjuan Stadium

UEFA Cup, quarter-final,
Leg 1: Sevilla 2, Spurs 1
UEFA Cup, quarter-final
Leg 2: Spurs 2 Sevilla 2
(Sevilla win 4-3 on aggregate)

The Lilywhites' adventure in Europe came to an end against the UEFA Cup holders Sevilla – though not without a fight. Spurs raced into the lead in the first minute when Keane stunned the hosts with a strike from close range and it was Spurs who looked the likelier to score again before Sevilla were awarded a fortuitous penalty on 17 minutes with former Spurs striker Fredi Kanoute scoring from the spot and Sevilla completed the scoring for the evening on 36 minutes when Alexandr Kerzhakov nodded home from close range. It was still a great result for Martin Jol's men who had every right to think they had enough quality to finish the job in the return leg. Yet within seven minutes of the second leg, the Lane had fallen silent in shock as the Spaniards opened up a 2-0 lead thanks to an own goal from Malbranque and another from Kanoute. Needing four goals to win the tie, Spurs understandably took an age to get going. It took 65 minutes and the introduction of Jermain Defoe to pull a goal back and a minute later the home fans went wild again as Lennon poked home the equaliser.

Spurs powered on in search of a third, but the mountain proved too great to climb and it was Sevilla who marched on to the semi-finals and eventually the final where they retained the UEFA Cup with a penalty shoot-out win over Espanyol.

PLAYER OF THE YEAR

DIMITAR BERBATOV

THOUGH there were several candidates for the Player of the Year award, there was only one really outstanding individual that deserved to win it outright – Dimitar Berbatov. His 23 goals in 49 games bear testament to his ability as a striker, but it doesn't tell the whole story about his efforts throughout 2006/2007 when he had the Spurs fans drooling for more each time he played. Berbatov is a prodigious talent who plays football the way Tottenham Hotspur fans demand – with skill, panache and he has the ability to do at least one thing during a game that will get everybody out of their seats – there is a word for it, of course – genius. In fact, so great has his impact been that he is already being compared to previous Tottenham Hotspur legends such as Glenn Hoddle, Teddy Sheringham and Alan Gilzean, all of whom possessed silky skills, vision and the ability to win a match on their own with one piece of magic. Martin Jol brought Berbatov to the Lane in May 2006 for what now looks like a bargain price of £10.9million, a fee that made him the most expensive Bulgarian in history. He'd become a legend at his last club, Bayer Leverkusen, scoring 90 goals in 194 games after signing as a 19-year-old from his first club CSKA Sofia. It's something of a mystery as to how he escaped the attention of Premiership clubs as long as he did.

Born in Blagoevgrad on January 30, 1981, Dimitar's father was a professional footballer for local side Pirin and his mother was a handball player - his background and younger years were very much sport-orientated and it came as no surprise that he followed in his father's footsteps by signing for Pirin, but his ability meant it was only a matter of time before a bigger club picked him up and, aged only 17, he joined Bulgarian giants CSKA Sofia. Oddly, he was targeted by a section of the CSKA fans after he missed a couple of presentable chances and became the target of the dreaded 'boo boys' as time went on. A move to Germany with Leverkusen was something of a relief to the youngster and though he had a slow start to life in the Bundesliga he soon settled down and began to show exactly why so much faith had been put on his youthful shoulders. He went from strength to strength in the next few years, scoring 46 goals during season 2004/2005 including five in the Champions League.

He moved to North London last season and began where he'd left off in Germany, scoring on his home debut against Sheffield United and ended the season with 11 Premiership goals and a further 11 assists. He was voted into The FA Premier League's Team of the Season at the PFA awards last April, underlining what his fellow professionals think of his ability, though it's the Spurs fans who are the real winners and much will be expected of Dimitar during 2007/2008.

YOUNG PLAYER OF THE YEAR

Aaron Lennon

There are a host of exciting young players at White Hart Lane and one in particular stood out during the 2006/2007 season – Aaron Lennon. The 20-year-old box-of-tricks had an outstanding campaign, playing 43 times and scoring five goals for Spurs, though he created many more for others.

It's incredible to think that he cost the Club just £1m from Leeds United in 2005, especially as he is now an England regular with nine caps up to the start of the current season.

His all-action style can be a nightmare for any opposing full-back and with his electrifying pace and vision, it's no wonder he's become such a huge favourite with the Spurs fans.

He signed a new five-and-a-half year deal in January 2007 and was also nominated for the PFA Young Player of the Year for the second successive season, but finished third after losing out to Cristiano Ronaldo of Manchester United.

Aaron was delighted to be voted Spurs' Young Player of the Year, however, and the Leeds born winger is looking forward to terrifying defenders at the Lane for many years to come.

He said: "I'm really settled here at Spurs and I'm thoroughly enjoying my football. There is a terrific spirit in the squad and we have everything to play for in 2007/2008."

IN FOCUS

MARTIN JOL
THE MANAGER

MAARTEN CORNELIS JOL was born January 16, 1956 in the Hague, Holland and began his playing career with local club Den Haag. He moved on to Bayern Munich in 1978 but returned to his homeland a year later to play for FC Twente, winning a first cap for the Dutch in 1980.

He then tried his hand in English football, signing for West Bromwich Albion in 1982, moving to Coventry City in 1984 and then moved back to his first club Den Haag a year later, collecting the coveted Dutch Footballer of the Year that same season.

Jol's coaching career began in 1991, again with Den Haag and his reputation grew as he guided them from the Third Division to the First. He later took on Scheveningen for one season, winning the national non-league championship. Successful spells at Roda C and RKC Waalwijk won him further accolades Dutch Football Writers Coach of the Year in 2001 and Dutch Players and Coaches Coach of the Year in 2002 – before he returned to England as assistant to new Spurs boss Jacques Santini. However, Santini's stay would last just 12 games leaving Jol to pick up the reigns as caretaker manager, a job whereby he immediately improved the team's fortunes earning him the permanent job of Head Coach. He scrapped the defensive style Santini had instilled and promoted Michael Carrick, ignored by Santini, to the first team. Carrick's inclusion was inspired and Spurs just missed out on a UEFA Cup place at the end of Jol's first season in charge. In 2005/2006 the Club then missed out on a Champions League spot on the final day of the season, finishing fifth and qualifying for Europe for the first time since the inception of the Premiership.

2006/2007 turned out to be a season of 'almosts', reaching the semi-final of the Carling Cup and the last eight of The FA Cup, but European football was at least secured for a second successive campaign with an impressive fifth placed Premiership finish and a brand of football never less than entertaining.

Jol's expert eye for a good player has seen some stunning signings in the past few years, most notably the arrivals of Darren Bent, Dimitar Berbatov, Gareth Bale, Pascal Chimbonda and Aaron Lennon and the 2007/2008 season looks like being one of the Club's most exciting for many years and with a fully fit squad and one of the most popular managers in years in charge, Spurs should be marching on, on, on!

PLAYER PROFILES 2007/2008

Paul Robinson

Date of Birth: 15/10/79
Birthplace: Beverley
Nationality: English
Height: 1.93m
Weight: 90kg
Position: Goalkeeper
Squad No: 1
Previous Club:
Leeds United

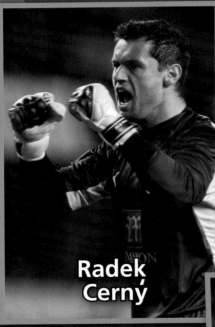

Radek Cerný

Date of Birth: 18/2/74
Birthplace: Czech Republic
Nationality: Czech
Height: 1.87m
Weight: 89kg
Position: Goalkeeper
Squad No: 12
Previous Clubs: Ceske, Cheb, Slavia Prague

Ben Alnwick

Date of Birth: 1/1/87
Birthplace: Prudhoe
Nationality: English
Height: 1.88m
Weight: 80kg
Position: Goalkeeper
Squad No: 17
Previous Club:
Sunderland

Pascal Chimbonda

Date of Birth: 21/2/79
Birthplace: Les Abymes, Guadeloupe
Nationality: French
Height: 1.82m
Weight: 75kg
Position: Defender
Squad No: 2
Previous Clubs: Le Harve, Bastia, Wigan Athletic

Lee Young-Pyo

Date of Birth: 23/4/77
Birthplace: Hong Chung, South Korea
Nationality: South Korean
Height: 1.76m
Weight: 66kg
Position: Defender
Squad No: 3
Previous Club: PSV Eindhoven

Paul Stalteri

Date of Birth: 18/10/77
Birthplace: Etobicoke, Canada
Nationality: Canadian
Height: 1.81m
Weight: 77kg
Position: Defender
Squad No: 7
Previous Club: Werder Bremen

Michael Dawson

Date of Birth: 18/11/83
Birthplace: Northallerton
Nationality: English
Height: 1.88m
Weight: 79kg
Position: Defender
Squad No: 20
Previous Club: Nottingham Forest

Ledley King

Date of Birth: 10/12/80
Birthplace: London
Nationality: English
Height: 1.88m
Weight: 89kg
Position: Defender
Squad No: 26
Previous Clubs: None

Anthony Gardner

Date of Birth: 19/9/80
Birthplace: Birmingham
Nationality: England
Height: 1.96m
Weight: 86kg
Position: Defender
Squad No: 30
Previous Club: Port Vale

**Benoit
Assou-Ekotto**

Date of Birth: 24/3/84
Birthplace: Arras,
France
Nationality:
Cameroonian
Height: 1.80m
Weight: 69kg
Position: Defender
Squad No: 32
Previous Club: Lens

Rocha

Date of Birth: 3/10/78
Birthplace: Braga,
Portugal
Nationality: Portuguese
Height: 1.83m
Weight: 80kg
Position: Defender
Squad No: 33
Previous Clubs:
Sporting Braga,
Benfica

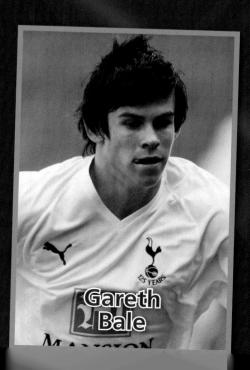

**Gareth
Bale**

Date of Birth: 16/7/89
Birthplace: Cardiff
Nationality: Welsh
Height: 1.83m
Weight: 74kg
Position: Defender
Squad No: TBC
Previous Club:
Southampton

Date of Birth: 14/12/80
Birthplace: Abidjan,
Ivory Coast
Nationality: Ivorian
Height: 1.83m
Weight: 78kg
Position: Midfielder
Squad No: 4
Previous Clubs:
KRC Genk, St Etienne

Didier Zokora

Date of Birth: 27/11/79
Birthplace: Tornio
Nationality: Finnish
Height: 1.75m
Weight: 69kg
Position: Midfielder
Squad No: 6
Previous Club: Auxerre

Teemu Tainio

Date of Birth: 18/2/83
Birthplace: Nottingham
Nationality: English
Height: 1.80m
Weight: 70kg
Position: Midfielder
Squad No: 8
Previous Clubs:
Nottingham Forest,
Newcastle United

Jermaine Jenas

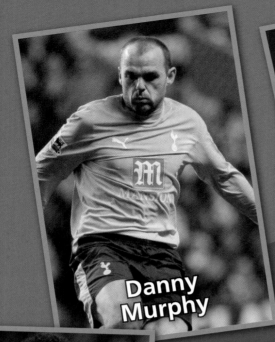

Danny Murphy

Date of Birth: 18/3/77
Birthplace: Chester
Nationality: English
Height: 1.75m
Weight: 80kg
Position: Midfielder
Squad No: 13
Previous Clubs: Crewe, Liverpool, Charlton

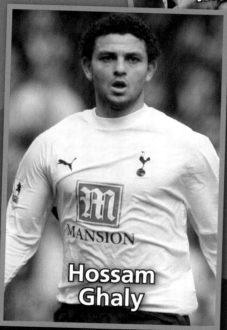

Hossam Ghaly

Date of Birth: 15/12/81
Birthplace: Egypt
Nationality: Egyptian
Height: 1.81m
Weight: 78kg
Position: Midfielder
Squad No: 14
Previous Club: Feyenoord

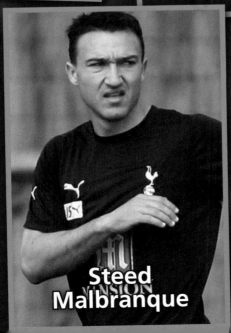

Steed Malbranque

Date of Birth: 6/1/80
Birthplace: Mouscron, Belgium
Nationality: French
Height: 1.70m
Weight: 77kg
Position: Midfielder
Squad No: 15
Previous Clubs: Lyon, Fulham

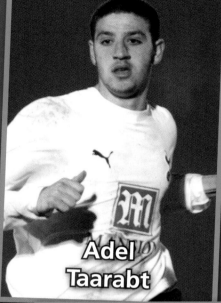

Adel Taarabt

Date of Birth: 24/5/89
Birthplace: France
Nationality: French
Height: 1.8m
Weight: 69kg
Position: Midfielder
Squad No: 19
Previous Clubs: Lens

Tom Huddlestone

Date of Birth: 28/12/86
Birthplace: Nottingham
Nationality: English
Height: 1.88m
Weight: 71kg
Position: Midfielder
Squad No: 22
Previous Clubs: Derby
County, Wolves (loan)

Aaron Lennon

Date of Birth: 16/4/87
Birthplace: Leeds
Nationality: English
Height: 1.68m
Weight: 63kg
Position: Midfielder
Squad No: 25
Previous Clubs:
Leeds United

Dimitar Berbatov

Date of Birth: 30/1/81
Birthplace: Blagoevgrad, Bulgaria
Nationality: Bulgarian
Height: 1.88m
Weight: 79kg
Position: Forward
Squad No: 9
Previous Clubs: Pirin, CSKA Sofia, Bayer Leverkusen

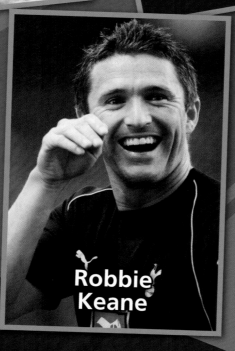

Robbie Keane

Date of Birth: 8/7/80
Birthplace: Dublin
Nationality: Irish
Height: 1.80m
Weight: 79kg
Position: Forward
Squad No: 10
Previous Clubs: Wolves, Coventry City, Inter Milan, Leeds United

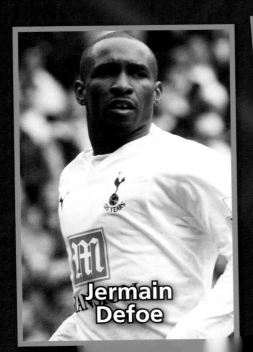

Jermain Defoe

Date of Birth: 7/10/82
Birthplace: Beckton
Nationality: English
Height: 1.70m
Weight: 65kg
Position: Forward
Squad No: 18
Previous Clubs: West Ham, Bournemouth (loan)

Darren Bent

Date of Birth: 06/02/84
Birthplace: Tooting, England
Nationality: English
Height: 1.8 m
Weight: 73 kg
Position: Forward
Squad No: 23
Clubs: Ipswich Town, Charlton Athletic

Kevin Boateng

Date of Birth: 06/03/87
Birthplace: Berlin, Germany
Nationality: German
Height: 1.85 m
Weight: 86 kg
Position: Midfield
Squad No: TBC
Previous Club: Hertha BSC

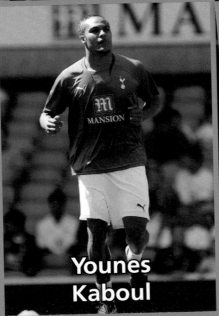

Younes Kaboul

Date of Birth: 04/01/86
Birthplace: Saint Julien en Genevois, France
Nationality: French
Height: 1.9 m
Weight: 87 kg
Position: Defender
Squad No: TBC
Previous Club: Auxerre

GET THE MESSAGE

Here are four mobile phones with text messages on – work out which Spurs player is sending the message and fill in the blanks

Doctor has told me not to celebrate like that again in case I hurt my back! Will think of something else for the new season, later
Robbie Keane.

I doubt I'll score another goal in my career but I enjoyed it while it lasted. Off to meet up with the England squad now, cheers,
Paul Robinson.

The lads are giving me stick for wearing gloves in the summer but I can take it besides, I can run faster than any of them! Later, mate,
Aaron Lennon.

Not expecting warm welcome from the Fulham fans! I won't worry about it and just try and score a goal instead. Catch up with you soon,
Steed Malbranque.

Answers can be found on page 61

TOP 10 GOALS OF THE SEASON

The official Spurs website asked supporters to vote online for their favourite goal of the season – here is a list of the 10 most popular strikes

1 - Dimitar Berbatov v Charlton, May 7 - 722 votes.

A wonderful individual goal from a wonderful talent. Dimitar Berbatov picked up the ball wide on the left, wriggled past two challenges before curling a delicious shot past Scott Carson – a goal Spurs fans voted their favourite of 2006/2007.

2 - Aaron Lennon v Chelsea, November 5 - 492 votes.

Aaron Lennon's superb control was the key to this stunning strike. He collected a pass, wriggled into space and then fired the ball past a helpless Hilario to send the Lane wild with delight and put Spurs on their way to a first victory over Chelsea since 1990.

3 - Paul Robinson v Watford, March 17 - 489 votes.

What looked like a simple free-kick upfield was actually an opportunity for Spurs keeper Paul Robinson to take an 80-yard shot that bounced over Watford's Ben Foster for a memorable goal for the England keeper.

4 - Dimitar Berbatov v Middlesbrough, April 28 - 450 votes.

The brilliant Bulgarian seems capable of scoring from almost any angle as this cracking volley at Middlesbrough proved. As Jermaine Jenas crossed to the edge of the box, there seemed little danger for the home defence but the elegant Spurs striker leaned back, connected sweetly and sent an unstoppable shot past Mark Schwarzer.

5 - Jermaine Jenas v Arsenal, April 21 - 388 votes.

With Spurs trailing 2-1 and the allotted injury time played, Steed Malbranque picked out Jenas 25 yards from goal and the England midfielder drilled a super shot past Jens Lehmann to send White Hart

6 - Teemu Tainio v West Ham, March 4 - 383 votes.

A super strike that befitted a super game packed with drama and goals. Berbatov played the ball to Lennon who spotted Teemu Tainio on the edge of the box. He back-heeled the ball to the Finn who hammered home a volley to bring Spurs level.

7 - Tom Huddlestone v Manchester City, December 17 - 298 votes.

The young England midfielder scored the best goal of his short career after running on to a chipped pass from Hossam Ghaly and volleyed a powerful shot home from 30 yards out. A stunning effort.

8 - Dimitar Berbatov v SC Braga, March 14 - 274 votes.

Tom Huddlestone aimed a free-kick into the Braga penalty area and Berbatov took the ball on his chest, spun and volleyed a right footed shot that left the Portuguese keeper grasping at fresh air as the ball flew into the roof of the net – and this effort only finished eighth!!

9 - Dimitar Berbatov v Besiktas, October 19 - 215 votes.

A stunning individual effort – again – from Spurs' Player of the Year. Berbatov received a pass from Keane and burst past his marker before turning the keeper inside out and slotting the ball home.

10 - Robbie Keane v Fulham, February 18 - 202 votes.

One of two almost identical strikes on the day, the second goal Robbie Keane scored in The FA Cup tie away to Fulham just edged the first. Mido flicked the ball on and Keane volleyed home with relish

CAN YOU SPOT THE BALL...

A

	A	B	C	D	E	F
1						
2						
3						
4						

B

	A	B	C	D	E	F
1						
2						
3						
4						

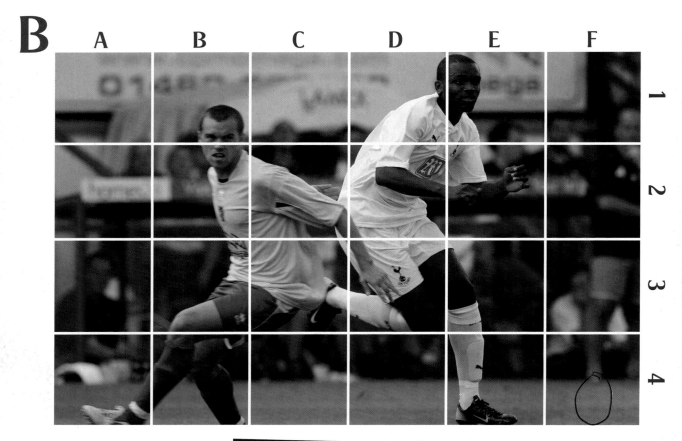

Answers can be found on page 61

WORDSEARCH

See how many words you can find connected with a matchday at White Hart Lane. Words can go horizontally, vertically and diagonally, forwards and backwards.

```
S C O R E B O A R D L H L
T N F Y K M S Y S T E N L
P U L Y L K K E F M J Q A
L S R R O F L L A E M T B
X C L N N B A L M T P R T
P A E G S G L M H I S F O
L R N T S T A L T T R D O
A V N N B R I C A E G U F
Y E U K G N H L N B P G B
E S T O N D R R E V P O T
R S R E T R O P P U S U D
S P M V V C H L W T P T T
V M X R Z H P L I G H T S
```

Answers can be found on page 60

IN FOCUS

LEDLEY KING
THE SKIPPER

KING BY NAME, King by nature, club captain Ledley King is the longest serving player currently on the White Hart Lane playing staff and the rock that Martin Jol has built his side around. A true Cockney – he was actually born in Bow – King joined Spurs in 1997 as a trainee and made his debut against Liverpool two years later aged 18. It was the beginning of a wonderful career for the 6 foot 2 inch central defender and his first goal for the Club was memorable in that it came after only 10 seconds (away to Bradford) and created a Premiership record for the fastest goal ever – one that still stood to the start of the 2007/2008 season! Excellent in the air, strong in the tackle and possessing blistering pace, King is almost a prototype defender – in other words, if you put all the assets and attributes into a computer to find out what an ideal centre half should be like, chances are it would print out a picture of Ledley.

He is also adaptable and played much of the 2003/2004 season in an unfamiliar midfield role with great aplomb and with such a cool head on young shoulders, it was no surprise when he played for England when still a teenager, selected by former Spurs legend Peter Taylor during his one game in charge as caretaker. Since then, King, who prefers to wear the No. 26 shirt rather than the traditional central defender number of 5, has been a regular in the national team squad, earning 19 caps to the start of the current campaign, though he has the likes of John Terry, Rio Ferdinand and Jamie Carragher all vying for the same position. He missed much of the 2006/2007 season with injury, but is hoping to lead Spurs to silverware domestically and in Europe this season as well as making an England place his own and his popularity was confirmed by a supporters vote of favourite players since World War 2 in which he finished ninth, higher even than team-mate Robbie Keane. Cited by his manager and Thierry Henry as the best defender in England, Ledley really is the King of White Hart Lane – long may he reign!

ROAD TO CARDIFF
Carling Cup
2006/2007

SPURS' CARLING CUP campaign began in emphatic fashion away to Milton Keynes Dons with Mido and Jermain Defoe both grabbing two goals and Robbie Keane adding a late fifth. A home tie against League One side Port Vale proved trickier than expected, but it was the visitors that went ahead and Spurs had to wait until the 78th minute when Dorian Dervite's flicked header finally beat Goodlad in the Vale goal. Tom Huddlestone and Defoe added further goals in extra time to set up another home time against Championship opposition. Southend proved a tough nut to crack and after 114 minutes of action there was still no goals – that was until Mido fizzed a ball across the box for Defoe to score the winner and maintain his record of scoring in every round. It had taken just three wins to get to the Carling Cup semi-final and the draw was the one the Spurs fans had been hoping for – a clash with Arsenal for a place in the final.

Things couldn't have started much better in the first leg, with Martin Jol's men opening a 2-0 lead inside the first 20 minutes through a header from Dimitar Berbatov and an own goal from Julio Baptista. The same player, however, scored twice after the break to complete an odd hat-trick and tilt the tie the visitors' way. Adebayor's 78th minute goal in the second leg looked like settling the tie, but a Jermaine Jenas free-kick found Mido's head five minutes from time and the Egyptian headed powerfully past Almunia to make it 1-1 and send the tie game into extra time. It was to be Arsenal, however, who progressed to the final with further goals from Aliadiere and Rosicky breaking the travelling

ROAD TO WEMBLEY
FA Cup 2006/2007

SPURS BEGAN their quest for the FA Cup with a tricky-looking Third Round tie at Cardiff City and the Welsh outfit provided a few scares during a 0-0 draw at Ninian Park. Goals from Steed Malbranque, Lennon, Keane and Defoe swept the Championship side away in the replay. Southend must have been cursing their luck when they were again drawn away to Spurs in the Fourth Round, but they couldn't repeat their heroics from the Carling Cup quarter-final and were comfortably eliminated 3-1 thanks to goals from Keane, Jenas and Mido. Undoubtedly one of the best away performances of the season came at Craven Cottage as Spurs turned on the style in a 4-0 victory over Fulham. Robbie Keane was on fire and scored two stunning 20-yard volleys to establish a two-goal cushion and Berbatov climbed off the bench to add two more sumptuous finishes to complete the rout. Spurs got the quarter-final draw nobody wanted - Chelsea away – but the Lilywhites came within an ace of a memorable win at Stamford Bridge with a stunning performance that had the Premiership champions rocking. Berbatov opened the scoring only for Frank Lampard to equalise but an own goal from Michael Essien and a solo effort by Hossam Ghaly left Jose Mourinho's side stunned, 3-1 down at half-time. Lampard pulled another one back after the break and Solomon Kalou broke the travelling fans' hearts with an 86th minute equaliser. There was still time for Defoe to rattle the crossbar before the referee blew to end a breathless encounter. The replay was another pulsating tie, but two excellent strikes from Andriy Shevchenko and Shaun Wright-Phillips proved an insurmountable deficit and despite a Keane penalty, The FA Cup dreams were over as Chelsea left with a 2-1 win.

ROBBIE KEANE

ONE HOTSPUR JUNIOR
THE OFFICIAL MEMBERSHIP

LILYWHITE & BRONZE
MEMBERSHIP 2007/2008

125 YEARS

JOIN *ONE HOTSPUR JUNIOR* AND RECEIVE A HOST OF BENEFITS INCLUDING:

- TICKETING PRIORITY OVER NON-MEMBERS

- AN EXCLUSIVE *ONE HOTSPUR JUNIOR* MEMBERSHIP PACK

- SPECIAL MERCHANDISE OFFERS THROUGHOUT THE YEAR IN SPURS SHOPS AND ONLINE

- ACCESS TO AN EXCLUSIVE AREA OF THE CLUB'S WEBSITE, FEATURING DOWNLOADABLE WALLPAPERS, SCREEN SAVERS, THE FANS' FORUM AND MUCH MORE!

CALL: 0844 499 5000 OR JOIN ONLINE AT: TOTTENHAMHOTSPUR.COM

IN FOCUS

PAUL ROBINSON
ENGLAND'S NUMBER ONE

WHEN PAUL ROBINSON scored that amazing goal against Watford last season, nobody should have been that surprised because he had done it before and actually began his football career as a striker! He used to lead the line for his school team but always looked handy in goal during warm-ups and knockabouts so when a new coach came in, 'Robbo' was switched into goal and he never looked back from that moment on.

Born in Berverley in Yorkshire, he was signed on as a youth player by Leeds United and he progressed through their Academy into the first team and made his debut against Chelsea in 1998, keeping what would be the first of many clean sheets.

He scored his first ever goal against Swindon Town in a League Cup tie, forcing the match to go into extra time and his two penalty saves in the shoot-out won the game for Leeds.

After 119 starts for the Elland Road club, he joined Spurs in May 2004 for a bargain fee of £1.5m and after just one season at White Hart Lane, the Club extended his contract to a seven-year deal such had been his impact during his first full season. Following a slip-up by David James for England, Robinson, who made his first apperance for his country against Iceland in June 2004, was promoted from second choice to play against Poland in September 2004 and he has retained the No.1 jersey ever since, playing every match of England's 2006 World Cup campaign in Germany and he'd earned 35 caps up to the end of the 2006/2007 season.

A rock in Martin Jol's side, Robinson is relatively young for a goalkeeper with so much experience of top class football and in committing himself to Spurs until 2012, he will join the ranks of White Hart Lane legends in years to come.

With no obvious challenger for his England jersey, he could well become one of England's greatest keepers of recent times and he found the perfect way to keep his rivals at arm's length when he scored that 80-yard goal against one of them - Watford keeper Ben Foster - in March 2007. He became only the third goalie in Premiership history to score – Peter Schmeichel and Brad Friedel being the other two – and he captained Spurs for the first time when he wore the armband against Southend in the Carling Cup quarter-final.

A terrific athlete and a magnificent reflex keeper, Robinson is one of the most popular players currently playing for Spurs.

IN FOCUS

DARREN BENT
THE YOUNG LION

DARREN BENT became Martin Jol's second major signing of the summer when he joined Spurs for a record fee of £16.5m at the end of June. The 23-year-old striker was raised in Huntingdon and attended Hichingbrooke School before joining Ipswich Town's Academy and quickly established himself as one of the Suffolk club's brightest prospects. He broke into the Tractor Boys' side as a teenager, making his debut aged 17 in November 2001 when Ipswich took on Helsingborgs during a UEFA Cup tie. He scored his first senior goal later that month against Middlesbrough, but it wasn't until the following campaign that he became a regular in the side, scoring 18 goals in all competitions.

Bent won his first England Under-21 cap in 2003 and in 2004/2005 he bagged 16 goals in all competitions and was undoubtedly one of the hottest properties outside the Premiership. It was no surprise, then, when Charlton Athletic shelled out £2.5m to take the youngster to The Valley after he'd made 141 appearances and scored 55 goals for Ipswich.

Bent made a dream debut for the Addicks, scoring twice away to Sunderland and winning the Premiership Player of the Month to boot. His stock continued to grow when he made his debut for England against Uruguay in March 2006, but when Charlton lost their Premiership status (ironically after a home defeat to Spurs!), it became unlikely that the player would be able to further his international ambitions while in the Championship.

He turned down an offer from West Ham, opting instead to head for White Hart Lane a few weeks later. Bent made 77 appearances for Charlton, scoring 37 goals along the way. Manager Martin Jol was delighted to have secured the coveted striker, saying: "Darren's strength is his stamina. Normally players will make runs three or four times in 45 minutes, he will do it all the time and if you manage to play balls behind the defence, he will be there. That's what I like about him.

"He has pace, he links play well and can see a pass - he can exploit the space and play as well. He knows Spurs is the place to be and that's something to be proud of."

Bent added: "Tottenham have a lot of young English players and we have a young squad - a squad going forward and that's the direction I wanted to take. Spurs seem to get better and better every season and I wanted to be part of that.

"It's exciting times for me and the club, hopefully I'll show what I can do at Tottenham and we'll go on from there."

🏀 HOME IS WHERE THE HART IS

White Hart Lane has been the home of Tottenham Hotspur for more than 100 years – here is all you need to know about 'The Lane'

SITUATED IN TOTTENHAM, North London, White Hart Lane is one of the most famous and much-loved stadiums in England and has been home to Spurs since 1899. It was built on a disused nursery, owned by Charrington Brewery. The Club rented the land and moved their offices to the new enclosure – a place that could finally be called 'home'. It would be 1937 before the officially registered offices would move across, however. The first official home game was played on Monday, September 4 - a friendly against Notts County - with Spurs winning 4-1 in front of around 5,000 fans. Five days later the first competitive fixture was played there in front of more than 11,000 fans, with Spurs beating QPR 1-0 in the Southern League. For 64 years, 'The Lane', as it had by that time become affectionately known, featured no advertising hoardings whatsoever – unimaginable in today's multi-sponsored Premiership! In 1923, the ground's capacity was increased to 50,000, though it was capable of holding even more, as a record gate of 75,038 fans squeezed in to watch Spurs take on Sunderland in a 1938 FA Cup tie. It would be another 15 years before

floodlights were installed to enable matches to take place in the evening – and that meant the cockerel being moved from the West Stand to the East Stand, though after so many years in one position, it probably welcomed a new view! Of the four stands at The Lane, the old West Stand was demolished in 1980 and reopened in 1982 and connects to Bill Nicholson Way.

The East Stand, built on Worcester Avenue, had three tiers and was designed by noted stadium architect Archibald Leitch in the 1930s and offered standing on the second tier, known by Spurs fans as 'The Shelf' until the 1980s and by 1990 the East Stand had been upgraded to its current condition. In 1995, the South Stand was completed to its current format and this also saw the introduction of the first Sony Jumbotron video screen, of which there are now two, one above each penalty area. In 1998, the North Stand (or Members' Stand) was completed and was the last of the four stands to have any major work. With a current capacity of 36,310, The Lane is hardly ever any less than at capacity on matchdays and with several

Premiership clubs leaving their old stadia behind to move to bigger, state-of-the-art arenas and virtually doubling their attendences in the process, its future is uncertain.

Whether the club does move premises or not in the years to come, White Hart Lane will forever remain the spirutual home of Tottenham Hostpur Football Club.

CAPACITY FACTS:

West Stand - Total: 6,890

North Stand - Total: 10,086

East Stand - Total: 10, 691

South Stand - Total: 8,573

YOUNES KABOUL

AARON LENNON

IN FOCUS

ROBBIE KEANE
KEANO

ROBBIE KEANE'S path to White Hart Lane was a long and winding one, but for the Spurs fans who have come to idolise him over the past five years, it was well worth the wait. Robbie began his fledgling career with schoolboy side Crumlin United in his home city of Dublin and he was soon being watched by a host of top English clubs including Liverpool, but it was Wolverhampton Wanderers he chose, reckoning there was a greater chance of breaking into the first team at Molineux – and his gamble paid off. He made 88 appearances in two years scoring 29 goals and earning himself a reputation as one of the brightest prospects in the country. So much so, he made his international debut for the Republic of Ireland in 1998 aged only 17 and has rarely missed a game for his country since. No wonder, then, that Coventry City stumped up a record £6m to

secure his services and Keane became an instant hit at Highfield Road, scoring 12 times in 34 appearances. His tenacity and skill had caught the eyes of clubs much farther afield than the Midlands, however, and in 2000 he moved to Italian giants Inter Milan for £13m – still aged only 20! Managed by Marcello Lippi, Keane was lined up to play alongside such world stars as Ronaldo and Christian Vieri, but Lippi was sacked shortly after Keane's arrival and the new manager decided not to play the young Irishman.

The dream move turned into a nightmare and it was a huge relief when Leeds United took him back to England, initially on loan, and he repaid their faith by scoring nine times in 18 games. Leeds had to pay £12m to bring him to Elland Road permanently and he became a huge favourite with the supporters, though his scoring wasn't as prolific and he found himself on the bench for some of the time.

With Leeds beset by financial problems, he was sold to Spurs for £7m in 2002 by then manager Glenn Hoddle who reckoned White Hart Lane could become Keane's "spiritual home" for years to come – and he was spot-on! Robbie picked up the Player of the Year award in his first two seasons in North London and added a third title in 2006. He quickly became a huge hit with the Spurs faithful and his partnerships with Jermain Defoe, Mido and Dimitar Berbatov – the latter earning a unique joint Premiership Player of the Month award in April 2007. He made his 200th appearance for the Club against Manchester City on the final day of the 2006/2007 season.

Still only 27, he has captained Spurs and the Republic of Ireland – for whom he has now earned more than 70 caps and is the all-time leading goalscorer. With spectacular goals, energetic celebrations and a contract that lasts until 2012, as far as the fans at White Hart Lane are concerned, there really is "only one Keano!"

SPOT THE DIFFERENCE

Can you spot the difference between picture A and picture B - there are ten to find!

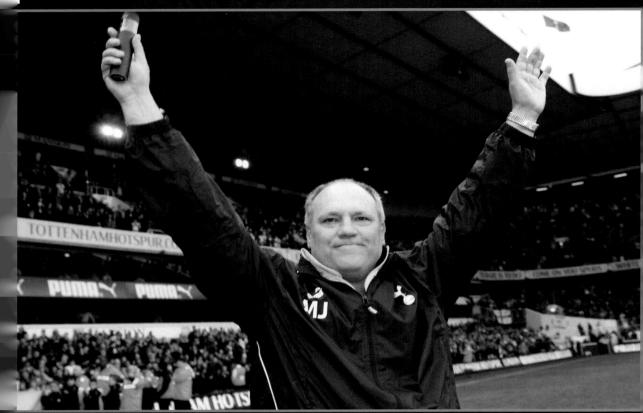

JERMAINE JENAS

THE BIG SPURS QUIZ

1. Which current Spurs player captained Canada in the CONCACEF Gold Cup last summer (2007)?

Stalteri

2. Name the two English clubs Martin Jol played for in the 1980s.

West Brom
Coventry

3. When did Spurs play their first game at White Hart Lane?

1899

4. Which team ended Spurs' UEFA Cup campaign in 2007?

Seville

5. True or false? Robbie Keane never scored a competitive goal for Inter Milan.

6. Where in London was Ledley King born?

7. Which north-west team did Spurs beat 2-1 home and away in the Premiership last season?

8. Which Spurs player made the shortlist of nominees for the PFA Young Player of the Year award 2007?

9. Name the club Paul Robinson, Robbie Keane and Aaron Lennon all joined Spurs from.

Answers can be found on page 60

10. Who is the former Spurs chairman that features in the hit BBC TV show 'The Apprentice'?

Sir Alan Sugar

11. Combining career transfer fees, which current Spurs player has the highest total?

Keane

12. Who used to play for a club named 'Anyang Cheetahs'?

Lee

13. Robbie Keane and Tom Huddlestone both spent time with which Midlands club?

Wolves

14. True or false? Paul Robinson scored his first career goal against Swindon.

True

15. Translate the club motto 'Audere est Facere'...

To dare is 2 do

16. Who joined from RC Lens last summer?

17. True or false? Spurs first ever kit was black and green.

False

18. Which Spurs player was born in a town called Blagoevgrad?

19. Which club did Jermaine Jenas and Michael Dawson both once play for?

20. Who was manager before Martin Jol took over?

TOM HUDDLESTONE

IN FOCUS

GARETH BALE
TEENAGE KICKS

GARETH BALE joined Spurs during the summer after becoming the focus of intense transfer speculation which included several other top Premiership clubs, but it was Martin Jol who moved in with a firm cash bid which Southampton reluctantly accepted.

Bale, an Academy player just 18 months ago, burst into the Saints' senior side aged 16 years and 275 days and only his former Academy team-mate Theo Walcott, now at Arsenal, can claim to have played for Southampton at a younger age. He made his Saints debut in a 2-0 win over Millwall in April 2006 and scored his first goal just four months later, curling a stunning free-kick into the top corner before celebrating with what would become a trademark twirl in the air. Sandwiched in-between was his first full cap for Wales and aged just 50 days shy of his seventeenth birthday, he became the youngest player to ever represent the Welsh after appearing as a substitute in a 2-1 win over Trinidad and Tobago – he also set up the winning goal for Rob Earnshaw just for good measure. He scored twice for his country during the Euro 2008 qualifiers against Slovakia and San Marino and it is likely Spurs fans will get to see a lot of his expertise from dead-ball situations in the coming years.

Born in Cardiff on July 16, 1989, Bale has won a couple of prestigious awards already, namely the BBC Wales Young Sports Personality of the Year award in 2006 and the Football League Young Player of the Year for 2007.

Assistant manager Chris Hughton said of Bale: "He is a good size and has decent pace. I am quite sure, looking at the type of player he is, that will also be quite flexible in terms of the positions he can play. I know he has been mostly used as a left-back, but we will see how his game develops. I see him as one who can play in a few positions."

With a price tag that could rise to £10m, Bale knows a lot is expected of him despite his tender years – but it doesn't worry him at all. He said: "Spurs are a club pushing forward, having finished fifth for the past two years. The young players here are progressing and the future looks bright with them doing well in the Premiership.
"It hasn't all really sunk in yet, but I am looking forward to it and can't wait to start playing."

GUESS WHO?

Can you work out the identity of these four Spurs players?

Lennon

Berbatov

A

B

C

Dawson

D

Jenas

Answers can be found on page 61

CAN YOU SPOT THE BALL

	A	B	C	D	E	F
1						
2						
3						
4						

	A	B	C	D	E	F
1						
2						
3						
4						

Answers can be found on page 60

2006/2007 STATS

■ UEFA Cup ■ Carling Cup ■ FA Cup

AUGUST 2006		VERSUS	COMPETITION			ATT
19 Sat	Away	Bolton	Premiership	0	2	22899
22 Tue	Home	Sheffield Utd	Premiership	2	0	35287
26 Sat	Home	Everton	Premiership	0	2	35540

September 2006

09 Sat	Away	Man Utd	Premiership	0	1	75453
4 Thu	Away	Slavia Prague	UEFA Cup	1	0	14869
17 Sun	Home	Fulham	Premiership	0	0	36131
23 Sat	Away	Liverpool	Premiership	0	3	44330
28 Thu	Home	Slavia Prague	UEFA Cup	1	0	35191

October 2006

01 Sun	Home	Portsmouth	Premiership	2	1	36063
14 Sat	Away	Aston Villa	Premiership	1	1	42551
19 Thu	Away	Besiktas	UEFA Cup	2	0	26800
22 Sun	Home	West Ham	Premiership	1	0	36162
25 Wed	Away	Milton Keynes Dons	Carling Cup	5	0	8306
28 Sat	Away	Watford	Premiership	0	0	19660

November 2006

02 Thu	Home	Club Brugge	UEFA Cup	3	1	35716
05 Sun	Home	Chelsea	Premiership	2	1	36070
08 Wed	Home	Port Vale	Carling Cup	3	1	34560
12 Sun	Away	Reading	Premiership	1	3	24110
19 Sun	Away	Blackburn	Premiership	1	1	18083
23 Thu	Away	Bayer Leverkusen	UEFA Cup	1	0	22500
26 Sun	Home	Wigan	Premiership	3	1	35205

December 2006

02 Sat	Away	Arsenal	Premiership	0	3	60115
05 Tue	Home	Middlesbrough	Premiership	2	1	34154
09 Sat	Home	Charlton	Premiership	5	1	35565
14 Thu	Home	Dinamo Bucuresti	UEFA Cup	3	1	34004
17 Sun	Away	Man City	Premiership	2	1	39825
20 Wed	Home	Southend	Carling Cup	1	0	35811
23 Sat	Away	Newcastle	Premiership	1	3	52079
26 Tue	Home	Aston Villa	Premiership	2	1	35293
30 Sat	Home	Liverpool	Premiership	0	1	36170

January 2007

01 Mon	Away	Portsmouth	Premiership	1	1	20194
07 Sun	Away	Cardiff	FA Cup	0	0	20376
14 Sun	Home	Newcastle	Premiership	2	3	35942
17 Wed	Home	Cardiff	FA Cup	4	0	27641
20 Sat	Away	Fulham	Premiership	1	1	23580
24 Wed	Home	Arsenal	Carling Cup	2	2	35485
27 Sat	Home	Southend	FA Cup	3	1	33406
31 Wed	Away	Arsenal	Carling Cup	1	3	55872

February 2007

04 Sun	Home	Man Utd	Premiership	0	4	36146
10 Sat	Away	Sheffield Utd	Premiership	1	2	32144
18 Sun	Away	Fulham	FA Cup	4	0	18655
21 Wed	Away	Everton	Premiership	2	1	34121
25 Sun	Home	Bolton	Premiership	4	1	35747

March 2007

04 Sun	Away	West Ham	Premiership	4	3	34966
08 Thu	Away	Braga	UEFA Cup	3	2	15000
11 Sun	Away	Chelsea	FA Cup	3	3	41517
14 Wed	Home	Braga	UEFA Cup	3	2	33761
17 Sat	Home	Watford	Premiership	3	1	36051
19 Mon	Home	Chelsea	FA Cup	1	2	35519

April 2007

01 Sun	Home	Reading	Premiership	1	0	36067
05 Thu	Away	Sevilla	UEFA Cup	1	2	32000
07 Sat	Away	Chelsea	Premiership	0	1	41864
12 Thu	Home	Sevilla	UEFA Cup	2	2	35284
15 Sun	Away	Wigan	Premiership	3	3	16506
21 Sat	Home	Arsenal	Premiership	2	2	36050
28 Sat	Away	Middlesbrough	Premiership	3	2	27861

May 2007

07 Mon	Away	Charlton	Premiership	2	0	26339
10 Thu	Home	Blackburn	Premiership	1	1	35974
13 Sun	Home	Man City	Premiership	2	1	35426

FINAL PREMIERSHIP TABLE 2006/2007

POS.	TEAM	PLD	W	D	L	F	A	PTS	GD
1	Man Utd	38	28	5	5	83	27	89	56
2	Chelsea	38	24	11	3	64	24	83	40
3	Liverpool	38	20	8	10	57	27	68	30
4	Arsenal	38	19	11	8	63	35	68	28
5	Tottenham	38	17	9	12	57	54	60	3
6	Everton	38	15	13	10	52	36	58	16
7	Bolton	38	16	8	14	47	52	56	- 5
8	Reading	38	16	7	15	52	47	55	5
9	Portsmouth	38	14	12	12	45	42	54	3
10	Blackburn	38	15	7	16	52	54	52	- 2
11	Aston Villa	38	11	17	10	43	41	50	2
12	Middlesbrough	38	12	10	16	44	49	46	- 5
13	Newcastle	38	11	10	17	38	47	43	- 9
14	Man City	38	11	9	18	29	44	42	- 15
15	West Ham	38	12	5	21	35	59	41	- 24
16	Fulham	38	8	15	15	38	60	39	- 22
17	Wigan	38	10	8	20	37	59	38	- 22
18	Sheffield Utd	38	10	8	20	32	55	38	- 23
19	Charlton	38	8	10	20	34	60	34	- 26
20	Watford	38	5	13	20	29	59	28	- 30

PLAYER STATS 2006/2007

PLAYER	AP	GL
Paul Robinson	54	1
Pascal Chimbonda	49	1
Young-Pyo Lee	31	0
Didier Zokora	47	0
Teemu Tainio	32	2
Paul Stalteri	14	1
Jermaine Jenas	34	8
Dimitar Berbatov	49	23
Robbie Keane	44	22
Mido	23	5
Radek Cerny	5	0
Danny Murphy	19	1
Hossam Ghaly	34	3
Steed Malbranque	41	5
Ben Alnwick	0	0
Jermain Defoe	49	18
Adel Taarabt	2	0
Michael Dawson	58	1
Tom Huddlestone	35	3
Jamie O'Hara	0	0
Aaron Lennon	43	5
Ledley King	27	0
Lee Barnard	0	0
Philip Ifil	2	0
Anthony Gardner	16	0
Benoit Assou-Ekotto	25	0
Ricardo Rocha	13	0
Dorian Dervite	1	0
Andy Barcham	1	0
Gareth Bale	0	0

ROLL OF HONOUR

Football League Champions 1950/1951, 1960/1961

FA Cup Winners 1901, 1921, 1961, 1962, 1967, 1981, 1982, 1991

Football League Cup Winners 1971, 1973, 1999

European Cup-Winners' Cup Winners 1963

UEFA Cup Winners 1972, 1984

Football League Division Two Champions 1919/1920, 1949/1950

FA Charity Shield Winners 1921, 1952, 1962, 1963, 1968 (joint), 1982 (joint), 1992 (joint)

QUIZ ANSWERS

THE BIG SPURS QUIZ (p 50)

1. Paul Stalteri

2. West Brom, Coventry City

3. 1899

4. Sevilla

5. True

6. Bow

7. Manchester City

8. Aaron Lennon

9. Leeds United

10. Sir Alan Sugar

11. Robbie Keane (£38m)

12. Young-Pyo Lee

13. Wolves

14. True – for Leeds United

15. To Dare Is To Do

16. Adel Taarabt

17. False – it was navy blue

18. Dimitar Berbatov

19. Nottingham Forest

20. Jacques Santini

SPOT THE BALL 1 (From page 57)

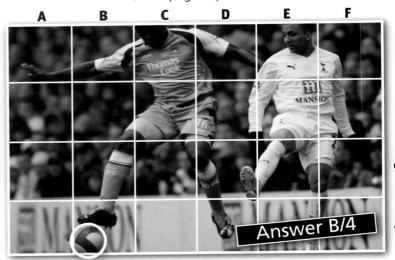

Answer B/4

SPOT THE BALL 2 (From page 57)

Answer B/C 4

WORDSEARCH (From page 31)

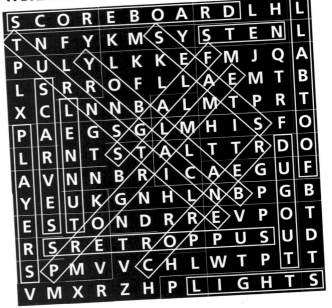

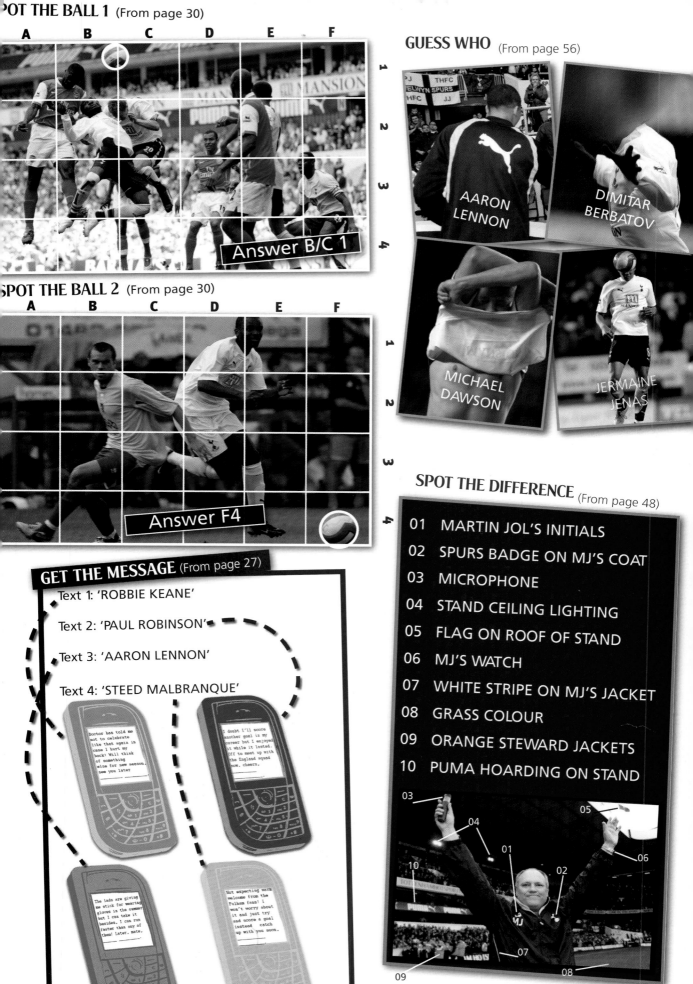

POT THE BALL 1 (From page 30)

A B C D E F

1 2 3 4

Answer B/C 1

SPOT THE BALL 2 (From page 30)

A B C D E F

1 2 3 4

Answer F4

GUESS WHO (From page 56)

AARON LENNON

DIMITAR BERBATOV

MICHAEL DAWSON

JERMAINE JENAS

GET THE MESSAGE (From page 27)

Text 1: 'ROBBIE KEANE'

Text 2: 'PAUL ROBINSON'

Text 3: 'AARON LENNON'

Text 4: 'STEED MALBRANQUE'

Doctor has told me not to celebrate like that again in case I hurt my back! Will think of something else for new season. See you later

I doubt I'll score another goal in my career but I enjoyed it while it lasted. Off to meet up with the England squad now. cheers.

The lads are giving me stick for wearing gloves in the summer but I can take it besides, I can run faster than any of them! Later, mate.

Not expecting warm welcome from the Fulham fans! I won't worry about it and just try and score a goal instead catch up with you soon.

SPOT THE DIFFERENCE (From page 48)

01 MARTIN JOL'S INITIALS

02 SPURS BADGE ON MJ'S COAT

03 MICROPHONE

04 STAND CEILING LIGHTING

05 FLAG ON ROOF OF STAND

06 MJ'S WATCH

07 WHITE STRIPE ON MJ'S JACKET

08 GRASS COLOUR

09 ORANGE STEWARD JACKETS

10 PUMA HOARDING ON STAND